# Mix Automation
## For the Small Recording Studio
~
## Sweeten Your Mix like the Pro's

Amos Clarke

Mix Automation for the Small Recording Studio
Copyright 2018 - All Rights Reserved – Amos P. W. Clarke

**ALL RIGHTS RESERVED.**
No part of this publication may be reproduced or transmitted in any form whatsoever, electronic, or mechanical, including photocopying, recording, or by any informational storage or retrieval system without express written, dated and signed permission from the author.

# Contents

Introduction .................................................................................... 1

What, Why, When, and How? ..................................................... 5

Micro and Macro Moves ............................................................ 17

Seven Basic Automation Moves ............................................... 23

Corrective vs Creative ............................................................... 27

Automating the Lead Vocal ...................................................... 39

An Automation Scenario .......................................................... 55

34 Automation Tips ................................................................... 61

Glossary ...................................................................................... 71

Thanks ........................................................................................ 75

Also by this author .................................................................... 76

# Free eBook
# Free audio examples

To my readers, I'm giving away my FREE eBook,
44 Reasons Your Mixes Suck - And How to Fix Them.
It's packed with common (and not so common) reasons why mixes sound bad and includes a solution for each reason.

Also, I'm giving away high-quality audio files that will give you real examples of some of the automation techniques outlined in this book.

**Please visit:
www.mixautomationfreestuff.weebly.com**

# one

## Introduction

What is mix automation and how can you benefit from using it in your mixing projects?

# What is mix automation?

Mix automation is all about 'sweetening your mix'. It's the final adjustments that the mix engineer does after achieving a good static mix, and it can significantly improve the balance, character, and vibe of the finished mix. Automation involves making precise, active adjustments to specific parameters on selected audio tracks. Because the automation is dynamic, each adjustment is repeated precisely each time the song mix is played back in the DAW. Typical parameters include volume, panning, equalisation, and plugin effects.

The simplest way to use automation is by altering the volume level of a track. A typical example is creating dynamic volume adjustments to a lead vocal track to ensure that it maintains clarity throughout the mix. Another example is where guitars can be panned narrowly during verses and wider during choruses. These examples are just the tip of the iceberg. As you become more familiar with automation techniques, you will start to find new and innovative ways to bring magic to your mix.

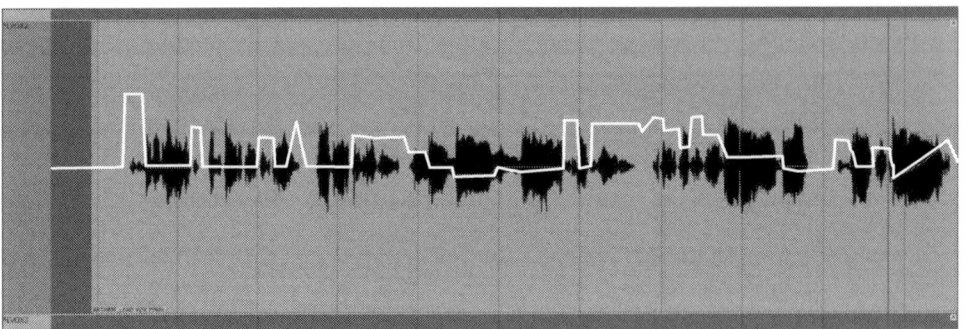

*Image 01: A lead vocal audio track with level automation*
*This image shows an example of fader level automation on a lead vocal track. The apparent random level boosts and cuts are used to create vocal intelligibility in the mix.*

*There's really only one rule
for using automation in a mix:
it must improve the mix!*

## Read this book if you want to:

1. Achieve very smooth and consistent levels of musical elements in your mix in a way that static plugins just can't match.

2. Create focus and interest in your mixes by continually emphasising different elements throughout the song.

3. Reduce the effects of frequency masking between similar-sounding elements by automating volume and equalisation levels in real time.

4. Achieve crystal-clear and perfectly intelligible lead vocals, no matter what genre you work in.

5. Apply unique and creative effects to musical elements in the mix.

## Who is this book for?

This book is for those who want to improve the quality of their mixes. It doesn't matter if you're new to mixing or you're an old-hand; automation offers a myriad of opportunities beyond what you can achieve with the set-and-forget method in your static mix. If you've dabbled with automation in the past, then this book may re-ignite your interest, give you new ideas, and provide a studio reference for you.

# How to get maximum value from this book

Let's get one thing straight: automation is not a magic pill that will instantly add that secret sauce to your mixes. Automation takes time and effort to learn, and time and effort to do. But the results are absolutely worth it.

If you really want to become a mix automation ninja, you need to take the necessary time to understand the concepts and spend time learning how to apply them. If you're a beginner, then read this book from start to finish and try out the techniques as you go. If you've got some experience with automation, you may find it useful to regularly jump to the tips section at the end.

Whatever approach you decide to take in learning these techniques, try and remember this proven method of learning: effective learning takes place when you first understand knowledge and then apply it. Follow this simple approach, and you're on to a winner.

# What this book doesn't cover

This book doesn't cover specific software packages, plugins, or DAWs. The information in this book is designed to be used on any system, regardless of whether you're using Apple or Windows, a laptop with Logic, or a digital mixing control surface with Protools.

# What gear is required to get started?

Most prosumer DAW software applications are able to do automation. Most half-decent plugins can be automated. It doesn't matter whether you use Apple or Windows, or a laptop or desktop. In most cases, whatever you're already using to mix music will be absolutely fine for doing automation.

## two

# What, Why, When, and How?

What elements get automated, when is it done in the mixing process, and how does it all work?

## What gets automated?

There are no hard and fast rules about what elements should be automated in a mix. Some engineers automate the lead vocal level only where others automate on a variety of tracks. A 2007 Sound-on-Sound article quotes famous mix engineer, Chris Lord-Alge, as saying, "I never needed more than fader and mute automation,"[1]. In another article, Greg Kurstin said that, "a lot of automation was used on the Lily Allen's vocal," when talking about her album, 'It's Not Me, It's You.'[2]

At the end of the day, what you decide to automate depends entirely on your interpretation of the song and your goals for that mix. If it's a pop song, then you may automate the lead vocal volume to ensure that it is always clear and articulate in the mix. Alternatively, if the song has many different instruments coming in and out of the song, then you may end up automating volume levels so that the mix maintains a reasonable level balance regardless of the combination of instrumentation playing.

The quality of the performance and recordings can also dictate the type and amount of automation required. A good example is for a vocal recording with extreme level variations; perhaps there are very softly sung parts combined with louder parts. Volume level automation would be used to raise the quiet parts and reduce the loud parts to give a smoother performance.

*The simplest and most effective automation move is the fader level adjustment*

---

[1] Secrets Of The Mix Engineers: Chris Lord-Alge, May, 2007, www.soundonsound.com

[2] Secrets Of The Mix Engineers: Greg Kurstin, May, 2009, www.soundonsound.com

## Automation can be applied to:

1. Individual tracks

2. Groups and busses

3. Sends and returns

4. The master buss

5. Plugins

**Automation and genre**

Often your automation goals will be driven by the genre of the song. It's popular for engineers working in EDM (electronic dance music) to automate a lot of plugin effects to create the ever-changing effect textures that typify that genre. If you mix rock or pop, then your attention may be on creating a great mix balance or maintaining an articulate lead vocal, using predominantly fader level automation. Alternatively, you might work in musical styles where you prefer to use automation as a substitute for compression to create a more natural method of levelling elements in the mix.

*What gets automated should be driven solely by your mix goals*

# Typical things you can automate:
*Note: some of these are repeated in detail in chapter 03*

**1. Precise (micro) volume level adjustment**
Achieve small precision level adjustments to the volume of a musical element.

**2. Broad (macro) volume level adjustments**
Create broader level adjustments to single elements, grouped elements, and to the entire mix of the song.

**3. Mutes**
Achieve instant silence of single elements, groups, and effects anywhere in the song.

**4. Fades**
Apply gradual or abrupt fade-ins and fade-outs of levels and other parameters.

**5. Panning**
Change the pan position elements in the mix.

**6. Alter the Equalisation**
Make elements more or less present during different sections of the mix.

**7. Dynamics control**
Alter the action of gates, compressors, and limiters.

**8. Control plugin parameters**
Alter the many parameters of a plugin.

# Why automate?

Perhaps the big question about mix automation is, "why bother?" Can't we achieve an acceptable static mix without it? Can't we just set those fader levels, choose our pan positions, and with an ample helping of dynamic and delay-based effects, leave it at that?

The main advantage of implementing automation into your mixing workflow is that it offers features and possibilities that give you massively more control than you can get with the static-mix approach.
This is why mix automation is so often referred to as 'sweetening the mix,' because it allows precise, dynamic control over almost every element at every moment during the mix.

From one perspective, your mix is like an amoeba which continually adapts itself to suit its environment. As more complexity develops in the number and variation of instrumentation, you find ways to adapt the mix so that clarity and definition are maintained. For instance, you might achieve great balance and clarity of the mix in the verses but find it diminishes in the choruses. This is no surprise as it's common for a chorus to have more instrumentation than a verse. And it's this addition of more elements that can reduce mix clarity due to the frequency masking effect of many musical elements playing simultaneously.

Because most of the concentration of musical elements occurs in the mid-range, the vocal (undoubtedly a mid-range element) often suffers the most. This, of course, makes sense regarding the listener; they will be less sensitive to a loss of definition between guitars and far more sensitive to reduced articulation in the lead vocal. This is a primary reason why engineers focus on maintaining lead vocal clarity in the mix.

## Emphasis and de-emphasis

The simplest and most effective automation move is to use volume level adjustments to emphasise or de-emphasise mix elements to create clarity and balance in the overall mix. Often the clarity of an element in a full mix is determined by the volume level of competing elements. For example, if your wonderfully articulate verse-vocal suffers from masking in dense choruses, then two things should happen. First, you identify which instruments are masking the vocal – let's say it's electric guitars. Secondly, you decide to either de-emphasise the guitar level or emphasise the vocal level – sometimes a bit of both works well.

In addition to being an excellent way to improve mix-clarity, the emphasis/de-emphasis approach is the perfect method to inject vibe and interest into your mixes. For instance, you can enhance definition by reducing masking, make a chorus louder, or emphasise a tasty guitar lick or drum fill.

*The simplest and most effective automation move is to emphasise or de-emphasise a mix element by controlling its volume level*

# 7 reasons why automation improves your mixes:

**1. Clarity**
The clarity of any musical element or effect can be improved by automating volume levels, pan positions, and EQ bands. For instance, a slight EQ boost in a presence range can add clarity to an acoustic guitar when it gets buried in the chorus.

**2. Frequency Masking**
Automating volume levels, EQ, and panning, are beneficial ways to reduce frequency masking between competing elements in the mix. Change the pan position, volume level, or decrease/increase a prominent frequency band to minimise masking.

**3. Texture**
The 'texture' of a mix refers to the character of the overall mix sonics during any part of the song. For instance, a verse may have a 'smooth' texture created by warm, swishy synth pads and less percussive elements, while a chorus may have a 'hard' or 'coarse' texture by emphasising transient-rich elements and distorted, gritty guitars. Automation allows the mix engineer to control the levels and accentuate varying combinations of elements so that the mix texture changes during the mix time-line.

**4. Vibe and theatre**
Automation is a useful way to impart vibe and keep the mix interesting. You can smash the drum room mic with a limiter during an interlude, raise the HPF frequency to give a radio effect on a lead vocal during the bridge, or feature a bass lick by activating a flanger for a couple of beats before a chorus. The opportunities to add colour and interest to the mix are endless.

**5. Establishing the Lead**
Establishing and maintaining a prominent lead element throughout a song is an essential component of most successful mixes because it provides the listener with a strong point of interest. While the lead element is usually the lead vocal in modern popular music, it can also be a guitar solo, a one-bar bass riff, and so much more. Automation enables the engineer to precisely control what the lead element is at any time during the mix. This topic is covered in more detail in the chapter, 'Corrective vs Creative'.

## 6. Consistent levelling

One of the most useful reasons for using volume level automation is because it allows the engineer to fine-tune the level of an element so that its volume sounds consistent to the listener. Volume levelling on a lead vocal is achieved by making small adjustments throughout the entire song. For example, quiet phrases that don't get raised by the compressor can be increased, consonants and fricatives can be accentuated to create incredible articulation, and vowel tails can be raised on the ends of words to keep them audible. This type of control is not limited to lead vocals; it's just as useful for levelling lead guitar solos, bass lines and anything else that isn't being adequately controlled by your dynamics plugins.

## 7. Mix balancing

Fader level adjustments on tracks and group busses can be discretely adjusted to ensure that the overall mix level and the combined blend of elements is consistent. For example, adding keyboards or a horn section to existing guitars could result in excessive level in the mid-range, requiring a minor level drop for some of the elements so that the combination of elements is still balanced.

*Automation enables the engineer to fine-tune the mix balance in a way that can't be achieved with a static mix*

# When does automation fit in the mix process?

Automation is best done after a good static mix balance is achieved. Ideally, the engineer would get the mix sounding as good as possible with all the usual panning, equalisation, dynamics, and effects plugins in place. An acceptable balance is often best achieved by focusing on the chorus sections first. Once all the chorus elements are consistently levelled, and in balance with each other, you can then review the remaining sections of the song. Obviously, any further adjustments you make to the other sections will affect the balance of the chorus, and this is where volume level automation is helpful. Applying automation into the other song sections allows you to rebalance these without upsetting the balance of the chorus.

You may find that once you have the chorus sounding balanced, you want to start automating. A common reason for this approach is to improve the clarity of the elements. For example, the lead vocal may sound balanced with the other instruments but may have lost intelligibility. Since the lead vocal is often such an essential element in the mix, it makes sense to implement fader level automation to bring back the clarity and intelligibility that is needed.

Lastly, avoid the notion that automation is going to be the big fixer for the trouble areas in the mix. While it can be an excellent way to fix small problems, automation can be time-consuming if there are lots of elements requiring remedial attention. Again, think of automation as a 'mix sweetener', rather than a 'mix fixer'.

*Automation is best done after a good static mix balance is achieved*

# How to create automation

**Old-school and new-school**
Automation is generally done in two ways. The first involves recording the engineer's physical fader moves on a console while playing the mix in real time. Subsequent playback should reproduce all the fader movements precisely. This only works if the console has motorised faders with read and write functionality. Before analogue consoles ever had this feature, engineers would manually make fader adjustments on-the-fly. This often required quite a bit of rehearsing, and at times, would involve numerous people working together on the console as the final mix-down was recorded to master two-track tape. They would repeat this choreographed session as many times as they needed to achieve the perfect final mix. But this process was not automation, but instead, the infancy of it.

For those who mix in-the-box solely, your fader moves can be recorded in your DAW in real time, or you can simply draw a series of lines or curves using the automation drawing features. In most situations, your DAW will automatically create the automation line for you, which you can later tweak to your heart's content.

Every automation line controls one parameter, and you can usually have many lines simultaneously automating different settings on a single track. For example, the line could control a track's fader level, the pan position, the amount of reverb from a reverb plugin, an EQ adjustment, a compressor adjustment, and so on. In many DAWs, the automation lines are overlaid on the track, so you have a visual reference overlaid on the waveform. There is also the ability to overwrite and edit the automation lines or disengage automation altogether.

The features available in modern DAW software allow significantly more control over the mix than the humble console. The ability to automate an almost endless variety of software plugin parameters means automating in your DAW is about as powerful as it can get. The great news is that nearly anyone with basic knowledge and skills can create world-class automation in just about any DAW package!

*Almost anyone with basic knowledge and skills can create world-class automation in just about any DAW package!*

## Summary

1. Automation enables the engineer to fine-tune and 'sweeten' a mix well beyond what can be achieved with a 'static' mix.

2. You don't have to do any automation to have a great sounding mix, but more often, it will introduce significant improvements.

3. Even a small amount of automation can work wonders on a mix. Many engineers will only automate the level of the lead vocal.

4. Automation takes time, but it pays off when it's done with a definite purpose.

5. There are no hard and fast rules about what should be automated in a mix.

6. Automating the fader level on a lead vocal is the most common automation move.

7. Automation can be applied to almost any parameter in your DAW or plugin and is usually as easy as drag-and-drop.

8. Automation is best done after a good static mix has been achieved.

9. Try and categorise all your automation moves into being either 'creative' or 'corrective', so that there is a clear purpose for each move.

Mix Automation for the Small Recording Studio

# three

## Micro and Macro Moves

Big moves and small moves: what's the difference and what do they achieve?

# Overview

Whether you are adjusting the volume level, panning, EQ, or plugin parameters, all automation moves can be divided into two types: micro and macro. Automating any element in the mix can involve one or a combination of both styles.

# Micro moves

Typically, micro moves are used to alter musical events that occur for very short durations. These include single instrument notes, excessive transients, and single words, consonants and vowels of a lead vocal. For example, the vocals in a verse alone could easily have a dozen or more micro moves to control the level. In this case, level increases could be used to improve intelligibility while reduction could be used to reduce sibilance and unwanted breaths. Other examples include levelling loud and quiet notes on a guitar solo and reducing fret clank on electric bass.

Besides being a great tool for correcting a performance, micro moves allow the engineer to get creative. For instance, you could add a big, long, hall reverb tail to the last syllable of a lead vocal at the end of a verse by using automation to momentarily activate a reverb plugin.

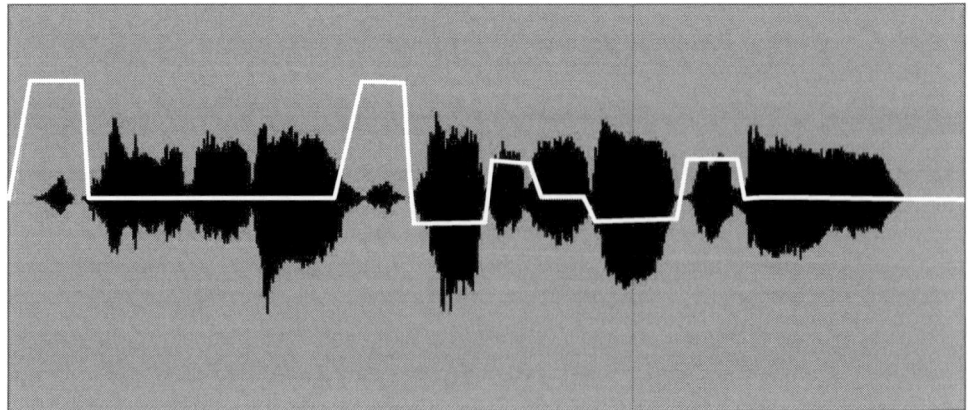

***Image 02: Micro-move volume level automation on a lead vocal track***
*This example shows how level automation (white line) is used to control the level of words and partial words in a sung phrase. The two substantial boosts increase the clarity of fricative sounds that are being masked (inaudible) in the overall mix.*

# *All automation moves can be divided into two types: micro and macro*

## Macro moves

Macro moves are generally longer lasting and usually have simpler shapes to their curves than the micro moves. They are used to alter entire musical phrases and song sections. For example, a keyboard track may need to be emphasised in just one verse, so a small level increase, say 1 - 3 dB, could be automated for the verse before returning to its original level. Similarly, you could raise or lower the level of an entire group of rhythm guitars for a chorus or increase the level of a drum room track for more room emphasis in a bridge section.

Macro moves are not limited to only volume level adjustments. They could be used to increase the level of reverb on a snare drum during a chorus, to mute an element, or to create a long and gentle fade-in or fade-out for an element.

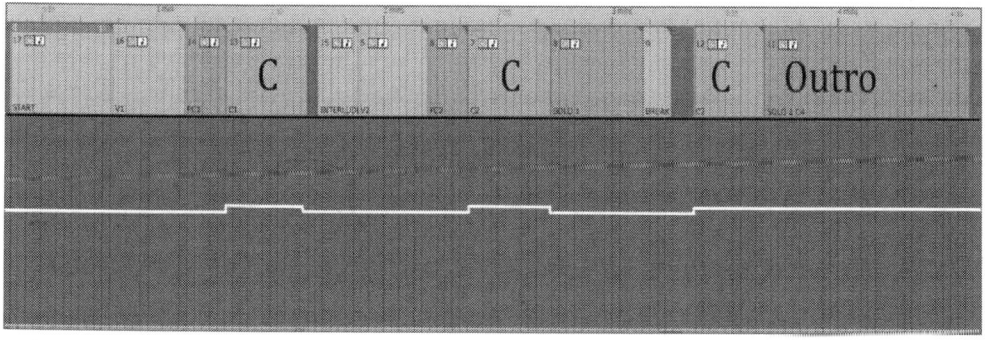

***Image 03: Macro-move level automation on the master buss***
*This example shows level automation being used on the master buss to subtly raise the level of all choruses by 1.5 dB. The 'C' markers at the top indicate the chorus locations in the song structure. Note the elevated level of the outro which is a repeating chorus.*

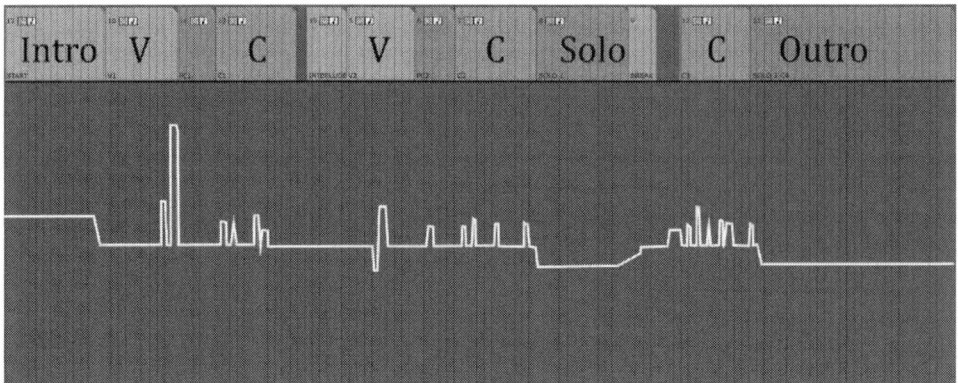

***Image 04: Micro and macro level automation on a rhythm guitar group***
*This image shows level automation on the electric rhythm guitars group buss across the entire song. Since all rhythm guitar tracks are routed to this buss, the level changes affect all guitars (note: this is not an auxiliary send). The goal of the automation is to control the level of guitars against the singing. Note how the guitar level is highest during the song intro before the singing starts. Throughout the rest of the song, the guitar volume level has a broad reduction to account for additional guitars added yet has short peaks that occur between phrases in the singing. During the lead guitar solo (the lead guitar is not routed to this guitar group) a keyboard is added with a corresponding level reduction of the guitar group. Almost all automation moves are in the range of 1-2 dB.*

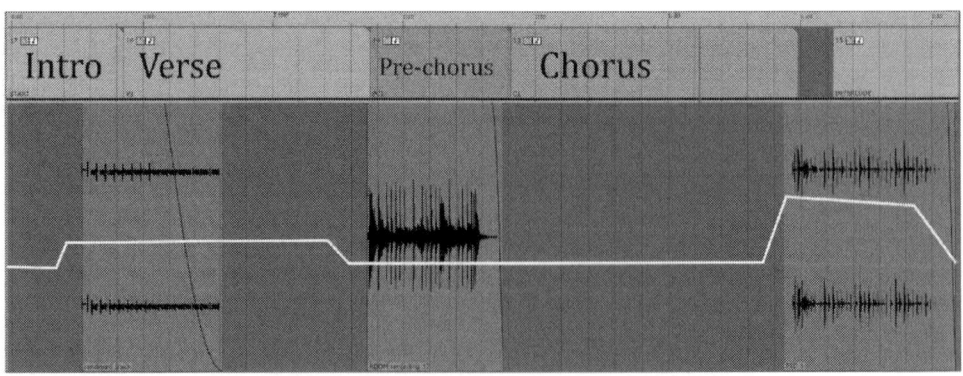

***Image 05: Macro automation applied to ambient samples***
*Macro-move, volume level automation, is used to balance the level of ambient samples in the mix. The volume level adjustment required is entirely dependent on the nature of the sample and how it balances with other elements in the mix.*

# Summary

1. Micro automation moves are short in duration and are used to make brief adjustments to parts of musical elements and effects.

2. Typical examples of micro moves are: adjusting levels of individual notes, altering transients, reducing unwanted noises.

3. Macro automation moves are longer in duration and are used to make adjustments to larger phrases and entire song sections.

4. Typical examples of macro moves are: raising the level of the full mix in a chorus, raising the entire level of a vocal phrase in a chorus, increasing the reverb on a snare drum in a chorus.

Mix Automation for the Small Recording Studio

# four

# Seven Basic Automation Moves

An overview of the basic automation moves you need to know

# Seven basic moves you need to know

Understanding some basic automation moves will create a solid foundation for you to develop your skills. The good news is that there are only a handful of techniques that you need to know and these will enable you to complete all of the automation work required in a typical mix. Some of the following automation moves have been mentioned in other chapters of this book. They are included here as a summary of basic moves you should know.

### 1. Micro-level control
Use micro volume level adjustments when you want to make very short, momentary level adjustments.

+ Improving vocal intelligibility by raising the level of vowels, nasals, and consonants (including fricatives and sibilants)
+ For an electric guitar solo, lowering a few overly loud notes and raising a few quietly played notes so that the solo has a more consistent level.

### 2. Macro-level control
Use macro volume level adjustments to raise or lower sections of a performance.

+ Raise the level of several consecutive phrases of a quietly sung lead vocal to achieve a more consistent overall level.
+ Lower the overall level of a group of rhythm guitars during a guitar solo to allow the lead guitar solo more prominence in the mix.
+ Raise the entire level of the mix during choruses to give them more impact.

### 3. Plugin parameter control
Adjust the level of any editable parameter in a plugin to achieve more control over delay-based effects and dynamics (compression).

+ Vary the signal level into a compressor to achieve uniform compression over a lead vocal with fluctuating levels.
+ Adjust the mix control on a compressor to achieve different degrees of parallel compression on a group buss or main mix buss – great for drums.
+ Adjust the delay or reverb level of any element.

## 4. Raising tails
Raise the levels of decaying sounds to make them more prominent in the mix.

+ Raise the level of the tail of the final note of a lead guitar solo to avoid it disappearing too early into the mix.
+ Raise the level of a decaying vowel sound at the end of a sung word.

## 5. Mutes
Achieve instant silence of tracks, busses, auxiliary sends, and effects anywhere in the song.

+ Instantly stop a reverb tail on a lead vocal at the end of the song.
+ Briefly mute an entire group of backing vocals.

## 6. Equalisation Control
Adjust the tonal character of instruments and effects to improve tone and balance, reduce frequency masking, and create emphasis or de-emphasis of elements.

+ Apply a high pass filter at 200 Hz to remove a build-up of low frequencies from a group of rhythm guitars
+ Using a parametric equaliser, apply a bell curve reduction at 3 kHz to remove harshness from a distorted electric guitar in a chorus
+ Using a parametric equaliser, apply a bell curve increase at 5 kHz to a kick drum to improve its presence during a dense chorus
+ Apply a high shelf boost on a drum room track to add high-end sheen to cymbals

## 7. Panning
Reposition elements and effects around in the mix panorama for fun or to create separation between elements.

+ Narrowly pan a group of electric guitars in a verse, and then for spatial emphasis, widen the panning in the chorus.
+ Pan an element to a new position to reduce frequency masking with a competing element in the stereo field.

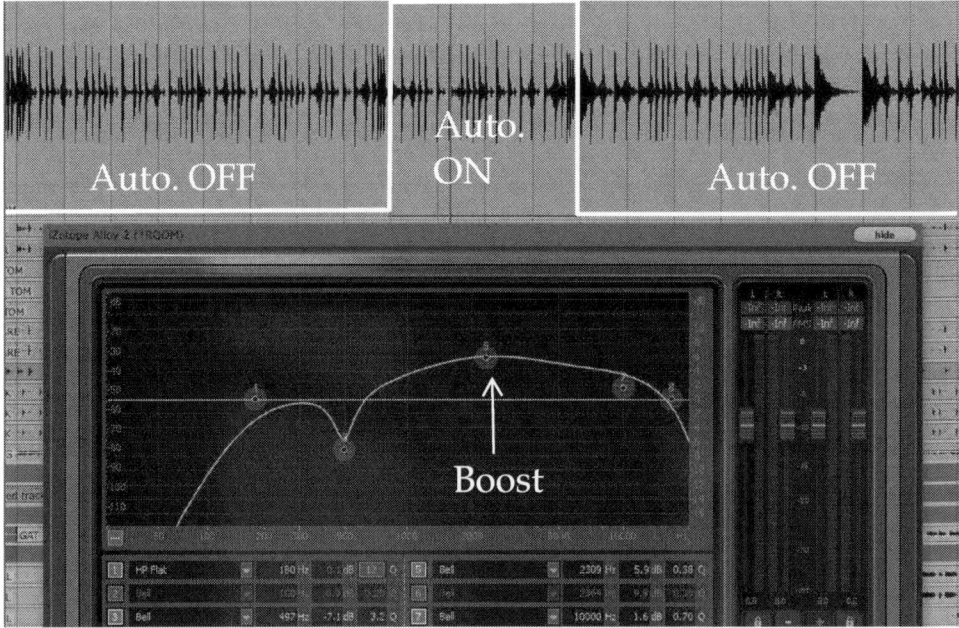

***Image 06: Automating an equalisation boost***
*Here we have a parametric equaliser plugin on a drum room track. A 6 dB equalisation boost is being applied at 2.3 kHz during a 4-bar interlude to give a trashy texture to the overall drum sound.*

# Summary

1. The seven basic must-know automation moves are: micro and macro level control, plugin parameter control, raising the tails, mutes, equalisation, and panning.

2. The most common moves are micro and macro level control. These are simple to use and extremely effective in the mix.

# five

## Corrective vs Creative

When to be a creator and when to be a fixer

## Overview

The goals for all automation moves can be divided into two areas: corrective and creative. Regarding workflow, it's usually best to complete all corrective moves before you start tackling the creative ones. Doing it the other way around is problematic; what's the point in getting creative with a slick combination of phasing and delay on a lead vocal, only to revise it later because you didn't attend to the corrective step of level balancing?

# The corrective approach

Corrective automation is all about fixing elements in the mix that cannot be adequately and conveniently corrected using static plugins. Most often, corrections involve level adjustments but also include equalisation and panning. Other corrective fixes can be done to control vocal sibilance, reduce over-bearing transients from bass plucks, or reducing the volume of harsh resonances in an instrument. But because the singing is so often an area of focus, let's look at ways of using automation to improve the lead vocal.

**Reasons you might automate a lead vocal level in a mix:**

1. You've applied compression, but quiet vocal phrases are still getting lost at points in the mix. In this case, you would apply small volume level boosts to give these quiet parts more clarity in the mix.

2. A guitar-dense chorus causes the vocal to lose intelligibility due to frequency masking. You could apply an EQ dip to the distorted guitars in the frequency region that is affecting vocal clarity.

3. Your lead vocal level is nicely balanced throughout the entire mix, but intelligibility is lost at some points. A practical solution is to automate a series of micro volume boosts to the consonants and fricatives.

4. Your vocal track is overly sibilant because the microphone choice was not the best for the singer. You applied a de-esser which is not de-essing all of the sibilant parts satisfactorily. You remove the de-esser and automate precise level adjustments to each instance of sibilance. Alternatively, you keep the de-esser and only apply volume reductions to the instances that require additional control.

5. The singer has a nasty mid-range resonance that appears when she sings loudly in higher registers. You tried an EQ plugin which negatively altered the rest of the performance. Solution: you automate the track fader to reduce each resonant note precisely so that it maintains a balanced sound in the mix.

## Adjustments in context

The level balancing of an element should always be completed in the context of the full mix. This is important because the engineer's aim when level-balancing a lead vocal is not how it sounds in isolation, but how it sounds in the context of the full mix.

There's a real temptation to adjust a lead vocal level in isolation because it's much easier to hear what you're dealing with. By all means, listen in solo initially, but get used to making your moves with the full mix playing. The primary reason being that the rest of the instrumentation can introduce frequency masking, level variations, and other things that affect the lead vocal's balance in the mix.

*The level balancing of an element should always be completed in the context of the full mix*

# Ears before eyes

Avoid making your automated volume adjustments based on the visual size of the waveform. The temptation can fool you into thinking that boosting the smaller waveforms and reducing the big ones will give you a great balance. While the relative waveform heights are a useful guide, it's a problematic approach. There are two reasons for this:

**1. The size of a waveform in a clip does not always relate to its clarity in the mix.**
At times, a larger waveform may get buried in the mix while smaller waveforms may have reasonable definition. The reason is primarily related to frequency masking. A larger waveform may be at a similar pitch to another instrument and get masked by it. Remember that waveforms show the volume level and not frequency information.

**2. The pitch of a sound can make it easier or harder to hear because of the ear's natural response to different frequencies.**
A waveform that looks small may be in a frequency range that makes it sound perfectly clear in the mix. Conversely, a large waveform might sound too quiet. Let's discuss the equal-loudness contours.

*Avoid making adjustments based on the visual size of the waveform*

# Equal-loudness contours

The 'Fletcher-Munson Equal-Loudness Contours' is a measurement of how well a listener perceives constant loudness across the entire frequency spectrum. The contours show that the human ear is sensitive to some frequencies more than others. While individual hearing ranges can vary, humans are most sensitive to frequencies in the 2 kHz to 5 kHz region, less sensitive to high frequencies, and least sensitive to low frequencies.

Frequencies outside the sensitive 2 - 5 kHz range get harder to hear as the volume decreases. In practical terms, low and high frequency sounds often require a significant level boost if they are to seem at a comparative loudness to higher frequencies. To add further complexity, your ear's sensitivity to frequencies varies relative to the level at which you monitor your mix. At low monitoring levels, the lower frequencies become much less audible while at higher volumes the ear tends to even out the level of the entire frequency range so that all frequencies sound more balanced across the whole spectrum.

The takeaway from all of this is that when you view an audio clip, you need to be aware of what frequency it represents so that you can make automation moves with the best outcomes.

**Making accurate and useful automated level adjustments requires two things:**

1. That you consistently monitor the mix at the correct dB SPL level (anything from 75 - 85 dB SPL depending on your mixing room size).

2. That you make judgements and adjustments primarily based on how things sound, instead of how the waveforms look on your computer monitor.

## What about Compression?

A decent compressor can provide adequate general-purpose levelling for most instruments, but it isn't always smart enough to do the perfect job required for lead vocals. Common problems are over-compression on loud vocals and no compression on low-level vocals. Compression can also emphasise things we don't want to hear, like sibilance, breaths, coughs, hum, and system noises. There are other factors at play too; the quality of the performance has a big impact on how well a compressor can perform.

While a good quality and well set up static compressor can get you a long way towards a well-levelled vocal, it lacks one thing: judgement. It also can't account for frequency masking from competing instruments. With care, you can make the necessary corrective adjustments to any part of the vocal recording so that it has the desired level of intelligibility with the correct emphasis and de-emphasis that you want for the mix.

This compressor levelling issue isn't just limited to vocals. Anywhere in the song where the level of an element seems too quiet or too loud, automation is the most effective way to correct it and get it just right. From weakly played bass notes and soft snare hits, to excessive transients from hot guitars, you can fix it with a simple automated volume level adjustment. And of course, if you only need to adjust one or two offensive notes in a performance, automation will give a perfectly tailored solution that targets only the problem parts. It's great to know that you're still smarter than a machine!

*A great sounding vocal can be achieved by the combination of a great sounding compressor and volume level automation*

But let's not be too hard on compressors, since some have a distinct mojo that adds character to a vocal that's difficult to achieve any other way. Also, a great compressor can get a musical element most of the way there in terms of getting a balanced level. A great sounding compressor and some deft volume automation can be a winning combination to get you that vocal sitting perfectly in the mix.

## One goal: different moves

An important aspect of level automation is that the engineer is making many different moves to achieve the goal of a consistent level throughout the song. However, there are times when automation is not the right tool for the job, and it's important to recognise this so that you don't sink hours of wasted effort into trying to correct something that could be achieved more simply.

For example, a regular sibilance problem throughout the song is best fixed with a de-esser plugin rather than individual level reductions for each event. Similarly, a harsh frequency band may be better treated with equalisation. However, with lead vocals there is often so much variation in a performance that a plugin with one static setting doesn't usually cut it. While the one setting fixes one problem, it can cause a host of others. For instance, your plugin de-esser might do a fine job of curing excessive sibilance, but it also can reduce intelligibility by quietening consonants and fricatives.

## Equalisation

It's not just level adjustment that makes automation useful. Equalisation adjustments are a simple yet powerful way to create a clearer sounding mix. For instance, the high-frequency parts of cymbals may be masked by bright, distorted guitars. A simple fix can be to automate a high-frequency lift on the drum overhead tracks during the chorus parts. Alternatively, changing the EQ curves can change the texture of elements in different parts of the song, such as getting creatively trashy by automating a mid-frequency lift to a drum room track during an interlude.

# The creative approach

With the creative approach, the engineer focuses solely on ways to use automation to add colour, texture, interest, and vibe to the song. A simple and effective method is to use volume automation to highlight certain musical elements momentarily as the song progresses. You could bring out a tasty electric guitar lick, highlight a single backing vocal within a vocal group, or fade in a musical interlude.

There is an endless variety of ways you can get creative, but the aim of getting creative is to introduce variation into the mix. This is particularly useful if, say, the verses in a song sound almost identical because of the same instrumentation. In this situation, volume automation could be used to emphasise, say, a keyboard in verse one, then highlight a rhythm guitar in verse two. Keep in mind that these volume adjustments are often only a dB or two; just enough to change the texture and inject variation into the mix.

*The primary goal of creative automation is to keep the mix interesting for the listener*

## Establishing the Lead

The lead element is, by its very nature, the most prominent element occurring in the song at any one time. The importance of the 'primary' lead element in popular music is that it is the key component that holds the listener's attention.

Maintaining a prominent lead throughout the song is a powerful way to keep the interest of the listener for the duration of the song. It eliminates the boredom that can occur due to overly repetitive song formats and arrangements because it continually highlights different elements as the song progresses.

Most songs have a primary lead by default, such as a lead vocal. A typical rock song would likely have two: the lead vocal and a guitar solo.

The problem with amateur song productions is that they often lack the necessary 'secondary' lead elements (also known as 'fills') that are required for a professional sounding song mix.

## *A well-crafted mix is generally comprised of a combination of primary and secondary lead elements*

These secondary leads are commonly brief moments of instrumentation that are designed to fill the gaps in a primary lead. The song, Emotional Rescue, by the Rolling Stones, is one of many perfect examples where the lead vocal ('Is there nothing I can say and nothing I can do?') is immediately followed by a momentarily emphasised bass/keyboard riff. The lead vocal closely follows the riff, and the cycle is repeated.

As you've probably already guessed, secondary lead elements can be any musical element. Most often, they are an existing element in the song that is emphasised, such as guitar riffs, bass riffs, keyboard lines, drum fills, horn stabs, vocal ad-libs, backing vocal phrases, and so on. However, having a musical element or sound effect that only features as a secondary lead can also add drama. At this point, what you decide to use as a secondary lead comes down to your own professional judgement.

The inclusion of secondary leads adds significant momentum and energy to any song. The takeaway here is that in many cases automation is required to raise the volume level of the secondary lead to give the necessary emphasis so that it's heard at a relative volume to the primary lead. Mix engineers can spend a good deal of time using automation to craft the secondary lead elements throughout an entire song mix.

Once you've decided on your secondary leads, you can add further enhancement by applying an effect. For instance, a rather plain drum-fill could be spiced up with a phasing effect, repeating delay, or heavy compression.

*Always feature one lead element in the mix at any one time*

## Delay-based effects, saturation, and dynamics

Using delay-based effects, such as reverb, delay, chorus, phasing, and flanging, can bring immense flavour and variation into any mix. You can add further vibe by automating compressors, limiters, and gates.

Automation is a great way to control these effects. They can be used briefly, such as adding a reverb tail to the last word of a vocal phrase, or broadly, like adding a flanger to the bass guitar for the duration of a bridge. It could also mean turning a radio effect on and off at key parts in the vocal delivery or raising and lowering the level of a delay on a synth in time with the song's tempo.

One potent technique is to create a 'transition' between song sections by automating a level ramp. The automation ramp can control a delay effect or the volume of an instrument. This is best done in lengths of bars so that it fits the song's tempo. For example, you can fade the effect in during the last bar or two of a song section. The effect then acts as a transition, cueing the listener to the next song section. Alternatively, volume level ramps can be used to gently fade out an effect, giving a very fluid sound to the mix.

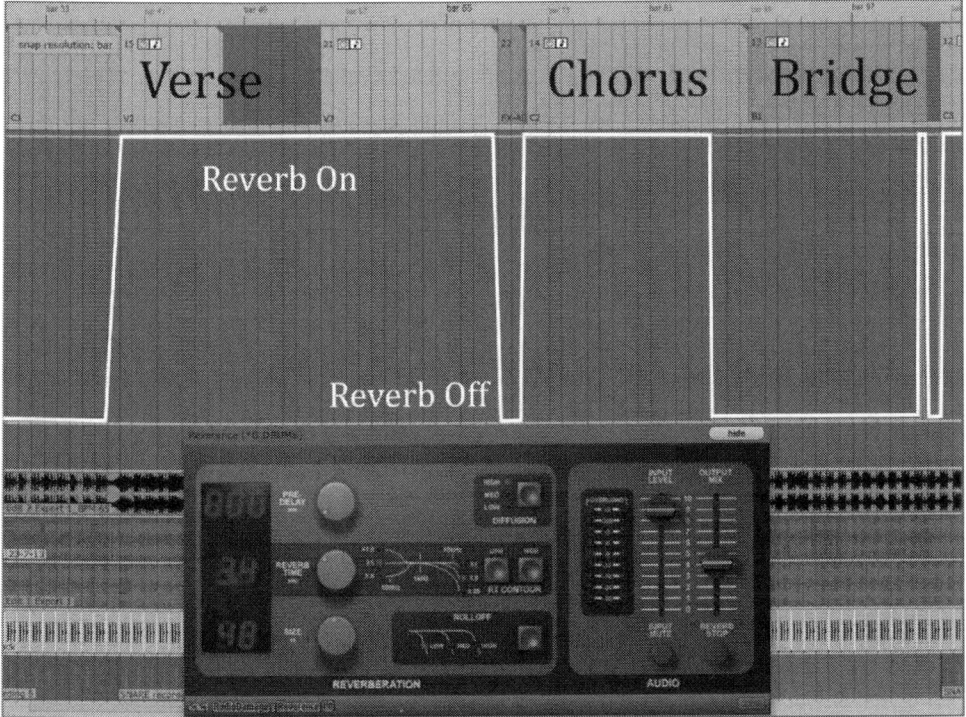

*Image 07: Automating a reverb plugin*
*This image shows a reverb plugin being automated on the drum group buss. The reverb is being turned on and off to give an exaggerated spatial effect to the drums. Note how the on/off locations align with the song format.*

Using harmonic saturation is a fantastic way to add grit and vibe to any song. Mild saturation can add body and thickness to a single element or group. Heavy saturation – or distortion – is an effective way to introduce character. For instance, you could automate a distortion plugin to add heavy saturation to some phrases of the lead vocal in the choruses or add distortion to the bass line for particular phrases.

Automating compression parameters is another excellent way to add vibe to the mix. This works by automating the input level into the compressor. If your compressor plugin has a 'mix' or 'blend' knob, then you vary the amount of compression that is being introduced to the dry signal. To illustrate this, you could apply heavy compression to the drum group, and then automate the blend parameter for more drum compression in the choruses and less in the verses.

## Summary

1. Corrective automation moves are made to fix or improve elements or groups of elements in the mix.

2. Creative moves can be any automation move that creates continuing interest in the mix by introducing vibe, expression, and focus to single or groups of elements.

3. Before doing any automation, distinguish between what is corrective and what is creative.

4. Always make the corrective automation moves before moving on to the creative ones.

5. Ensure that you make your final automation moves with the full mix playing so that your moves can be heard in the context of the full mix. Avoid making your final moves in solo mode.

6. Use your ears when making automation moves and avoid making judgements solely based on the visual size of the waveform on your screen.

# six

## Automating the Lead Vocal

Let's focus on arguably the most essential element to automate

# The importance of vocal intelligibility

If there is one single element that should get the mix engineer's attention for automating, it's the lead vocal. Since the human ear is so well tuned to voice, it's natural for listeners to notice when speech or singing loses intelligibility and clarity in a song; listeners quickly become aware when the communication of the story is lost.

In many cases, automating the vocal's track fader level will be the most effective method to achieve intelligibility in the mix. And as stated earlier, it's the subtle micro-moves that are most effective. The rest of this chapter will focus on how automation can be used to do all sorts of corrective and creative tricks to get your vocal to shine in the mix.

When a vocal becomes less intelligible in the mix, the obvious solution is to raise the overall fader level to make it more prominent, but this can throw the mix out of balance, leaving other elements sounding weak in comparison. Raising the vocal level can also cause frequency masking, reducing the definition of other competing mid-range elements such as guitars, pianos, and backing vocals. Genres such as hard rock and metal, require the vocal to sit relatively low in the mix; setting a high vocal level to achieve clarity can destroy the mixing style that the genre demands. Automation allows you to settle that vocal down into the mix to create a better overall balance, then use a combination of automation moves to bring back the clarity and definition.

The importance of vocal intelligibility varies between genres and because of this, the automation requirements will differ as well. Is it critical to understand every word in Death Metal? Probably not since the Death Metal genre is more about expressing musical groove and energy and less about telling stories. If listeners, due to a lack of intelligibility, can't understand the words in a song by Adele or Ed Sheeran, they'll be disappointed. Rap music is similar because the vocal delivery is often a fast-paced story and if the audience can't understand the story, the song suffers. For genres whose success rely on telling a story – and so many music styles do – vocal clarity and intelligibility are critical to the success of the song.

*Automating the volume level is the simplest and most effective method to achieve intelligibility in the mix*

## The primary goals for automating a lead vocal:

### 1. Creating vocal intelligibility:
Vocal intelligibility is clear due to the prominence of consonants, nasals, fricatives, and vowels. Listeners can hear and understand the lyrics.

### 2. Creating a relative vocal balance:
The vocal has a good comparative level balance in comparison to the other musical elements playing in the mix. Depending on the genre, the lead vocal may be slightly up or down in the mix.

### 3. Creating vocal character:
The vocal's tonal character can be altered by automating level, dynamics, and delay-based effects.

Each of these three goals is discussed below.

# 1. Creating vocal intelligibility

## Consistent Level

Volume level automation is the most straightforward automation technique for creating a consistently levelled lead vocal. To achieve this requires a combination of micro and macro moves. To do this accurately and effectively needs you to make all your moves with the entire mix playing, rather than with the track soloed. Further refinement can be achieved by applying automation in mono at very low volume levels - this technique makes vocal level fluctuations, and clarity pronounced compared to listening at higher volumes on full range stereo monitoring.

With any recording performance, it's common for vocalists to sing phrases and words at different volumes. Sometimes it's a result of poor singing technique while at other times these level variations are merely part of the performance, like softly sung verses and more intensely sung choruses. While such delivery might sound fine in isolation, the level variations can cause the vocals to disappear into the mix or become overly loud, depending on what other instrumentation is playing.

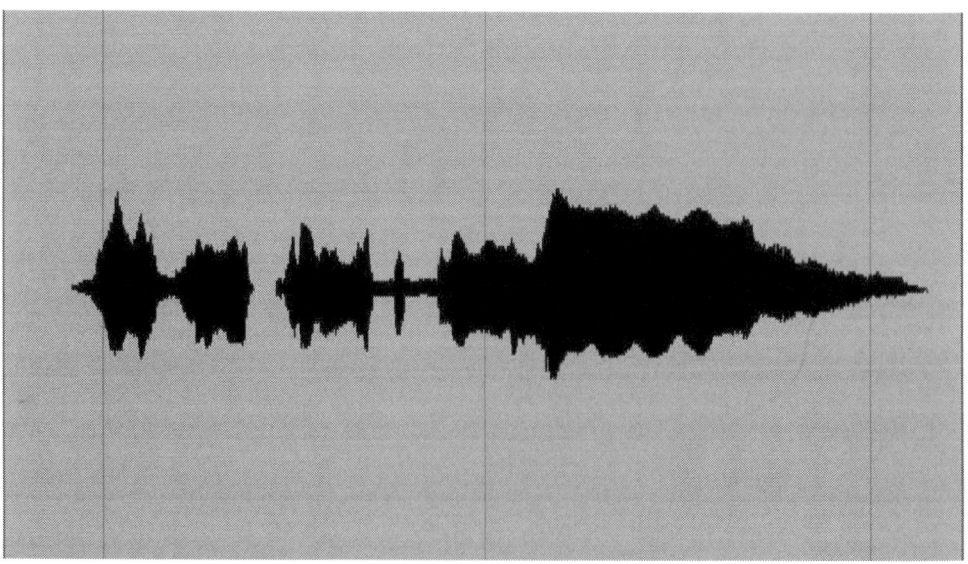

***Image 08: The level variations within a lead vocal recording***
*This image shows the level variations in a sung phrase.*

In many cases, a compressor will level a vocal adequately, but different types affect a vocal differently, and they can introduce unsavoury audible artefacts that require further processing to fix. Examples are accentuated sibilance and transients, distortion, and raising the noise floor. Additionally, unless you automate the compressors threshold and output level, the low-level vocals may not trigger compression, while the loud parts can cause over-compression.

When a singer delivers outside their normal vocal range, they tend to expel less air. Therefore, the recorded level of a vocal can vary depending on the frequency it is sung. A vocalist singing in a low (vocal fry) register and falsetto are typical examples of this. The outcome is that there is often a need to adjust these fluctuating levels in the mix.

Some female singers can sound very resonant in particular frequency ranges. It's not uncommon to hear this in the upper mid-range when they're singing loudly. Since the human ear is very sensitive in the 3 – 5 kHz frequency range, vocal resonances in this zone can become quite uncomfortable for the listener and seem out of balance in the mix. This issue can sometimes be fixed using a static, dynamic equaliser but is better achieved by automating a volume level or EQ reduction in the offending region. This method allows the engineer precise control over each occurrence of the resonance.

## Achieving vocal intelligibility in the mix

The trick to achieving vocal intelligibility in the mix goes beyond applying a broad level boost. An intelligible vocal is characterised by particular features referred to as 'the elements of articulation'. Each of these elements has a specific sound character in a sung vocal. Depending on the singer, the performance, the vocal recording chain, and competing elements in the mix, these articulation elements can require corrective automation to optimise their intelligibility in the mix. The elements of articulation consist of vowels, nasals, and consonants. When the mixing engineer is familiar with the sound of these articulation elements, he or she can optimise their processing to suit.

The mix processing and automation that could typically be done on a lead vocal depends on whether the goal is to be corrective, creative, or both. And again, depending on the quality of the recording, the processing requirements could be anything from minimal to major.

For example, if the recording capture is of good quality and the mix engineer is only looking to take the corrective approach and aim for consistent level, a compressor and some minor level automation may be all that is required. For the automation, the levelling would target each of the three articulation elements to ensure that each has a controlled clarity in the mix. An experienced engineer may look to reduce sibilance and overly loud words, while aiming to boost nasals, soft fricatives, and the tails of vowels.

Achieving this degree of automation control requires you to identify every instance and make the appropriate level adjustment. While this may seem arduous, it's an almost guaranteed method of achieving a superb sounding lead vocal that is clear and present in the mix.

## Vocal elements of articulation
*Note: the following explanations have been simplified to avoid a complicated and distracting discussion about articulation.*

### Vowels:
Vowel sounds consist of the standard alphabetical vowels: a, e, i, o, and u. These are mostly open, sustained sounds, such as the A in Behave, the O Lose, the I in Mile, and the U in Mule. They also include shorter, more percussive sounds like the I In and the U in But. However, with all vowel sounds, the amount of emphasis and sustain depends on the phrasing delivered by the singer.

### Nasals:
Nasal sounds are those that are made predominantly through the nose and mainly include M and N sounds. Examples are the M in Boom and the NG in Song. However, vowel sounds can become nasal depending on how the vocalist chooses to sing them.

### Consonants (including fricatives and sibilants):
Consonants include all the alphabetical sounds that are not vowels. They are the most complex to discuss since they include fricatives and sibilants and each of these has a different sound that can require different treatment in the mix.

Regarding achieving mix clarity, the engineer can simplify consonants into three categories: hard consonants, fricatives, and sibilants. Examples of hard consonants include the M in Mat, the C in Cat, the P in Pop, the T in Take, the B in Bag, the L in Lake, and so on.

Fricatives (officially called fricative consonants) are a form of soft consonant created by forcing air through a narrow passage in the mouth, creating a 'wishy' noise. Examples are, the F in Find, the J in Judge, the G in Manager, the Sh in Welsh, and the Ch in Chicken. Fricatives often require a level boost, especially in dense mixes, since when inaudible, they significantly reduce the intelligibility of sung words.

Sibilants are a subset of fricatives, where a pronounced hissing sound is created. These include the S in Sound, the Z in Zip, and the X in Six. There is some debate about the difference between particular fricatives and sibilants; a disagreement that is distracting and unhelpful in this book. The main takeaway about sibilants is that, due to their intensity, they often require a level reduction in the mix. Again, this is dictated by the singer's performance and the recording chain (many consumer-level vocal microphones accentuate the sibilance).

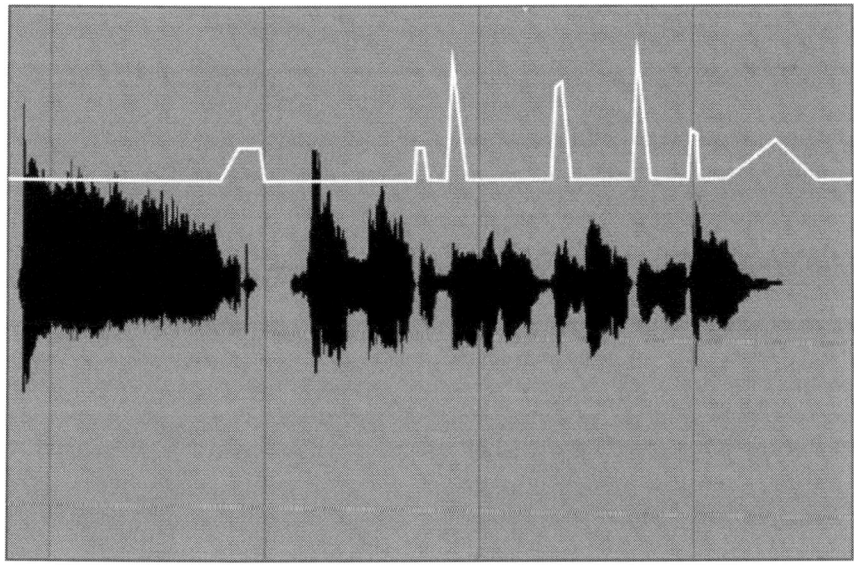

***Image 09: Micro volume level automation applied to a lead vocal***
*In this sung phrase, micro level automation is being used to emphasise (mainly) the first consonant of most of the words so that the vocals have a slightly aggressive style of enunciation and sound very clear in the overall mix.*

In a typical song mix, vowel sounds are usually a lot easier to control than sibilants and fricatives when considering vocal intelligibility. This is mainly because vowels are often held for longer and also because the surrounding consonants in a word can help the brain fill in the gaps if the vowel is not so prominent. However, vowel clarity can be affected by frequency masking from other instruments so you may find that a slight level boost will avoid the vowel being masked. When a word tail ends in a vowel, these are often lost in the mix. A simple fix is to automate a volume level swell as the vowel tail is decaying at the end of the word.

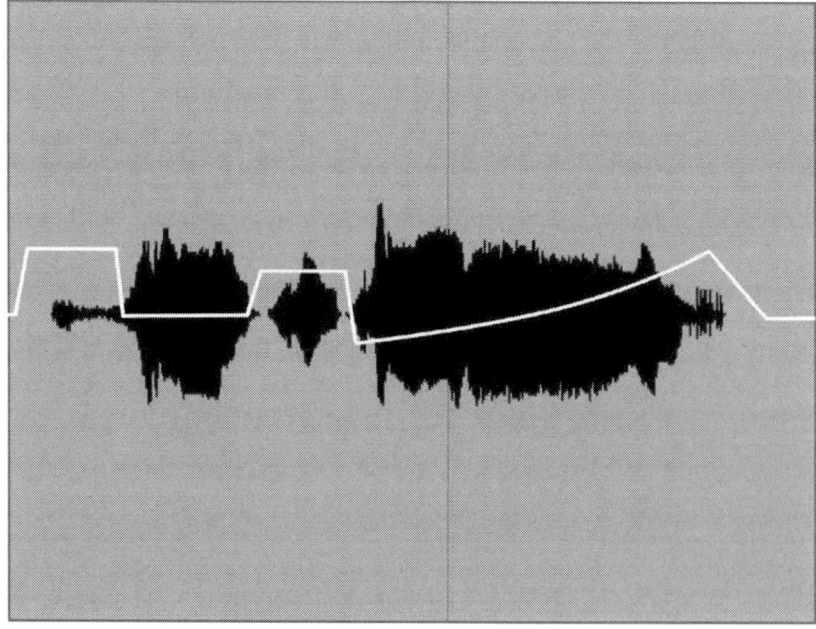

*Image 10: Volume level automation applied to a lead vocal*
*Volume level automation is applied to a lead vocal phrase. Note the big boost to the fricative at the start and also the gradual level increase applied to the vowel tail to prevent it becoming inaudible in the mix. The softly sung fricative at the end of the vowel also benefits from a boost.*

## Equalisation automation on the lead vocal

Automating an equaliser is another extremely effective way to bring clarity and intelligibility to a vocal. But why do this when we could keep it simple and just automate the level?

There are many situations when a vocal is well balanced with other mix elements, but it loses intelligibility during dense song sections because of frequency masking from competing elements. While raising the level of the masked words can improve the vocal, it can also put the vocal out of balance in the mix. Automating an equaliser can be a better alternative to volume level automation because you're only adjusting the level of a limited range of the frequency spectrum.

If you want to improve vocal intelligibility by automating an equaliser, then focusing on the mid/ high-frequency range is often effective by targeting frequencies from 5 kHz to around 8 kHz. Usually, the equalisation adjustment need only be a dB or two and activated just for the duration of the song section.

Another useful frequency point for improving vocal clarity is the 10 kHz range. Automating a few dB lift with a relatively broad bell curve can add a glassy sheen, or 'air', that can add a wonderful presence. Be aware that boosts within and just below this range can increase sibilance.

A high pass filter (HPF) can work wonders if the lower notes of the vocal are losing clarity due to masking. Again, if more instruments are introduced that have energy in the low range - like guitars, horns and keyboards – vocal clarity can suffer. This is particularly noticeable for vowel sounds that have their fundamental frequency in the range of the competing instrument. In this situation, automating an HPF with a shallow slope on the vocal at around 200 Hz can help solve this. Of course, the roll-off frequency will vary depending on the vocal and the instrumentation. Choosing your roll-off point can be a delicate operation because the aim is to reduce the masking yet maintain vocal clarity. An alternative solution is to apply an HPF to the instruments, which will leave the vocal unaffected.

One drawback to EQing vocals is that excessive adjustments can affect the natural character of a vocal. It's not only vocal clarity that is quickly noticed by an audience; listeners can easily detect when the human voice sounds weird or unnatural. Therefore, it can be a good idea to apply equalisation to a vocal that will retain a natural tonality while focusing more dramatic EQ moves on the competing instruments.

*A great balance requires control over the levels of multiple musical elements simultaneously so that all can be heard, yet each has the appropriate degree of prominence in the mix*

## Complementary equalisation

This method requires the engineer to make equalisation adjustments to two or more similar sounding musical elements that coincide in the mix. The goal is to create more definition and separation between them so that they can be heard more as individual elements in the mix. Clearly this can be tricky when you're trying to achieve distinction between, say, two almost identical sounding distorted electric guitars. To do this, you make one or more subtle equalisation adjustments to one element, then make the opposite adjustment on the other element. In other words, adding a 1.5 dB boost at 120 Hz on one guitar would have you making a complementary 1.5 dB dip at 120 Hz to the other guitar.

**Examples of complementary EQ applications:**

1. The left and right drum overhead tracks.
2. A kick drum and bass guitar.
3. Two similar-sounding electric guitars.
4. Two acoustic guitars.
5. Lead vocals and backing vocals.

The option to activate complementary EQ on and off using automation offers many advantages in how an engineer can use EQ in the mix. With a static mix, your complementary EQ adjustments are activated for the entire mix, which can be problematic if you just want it enabled in specific parts of the song.

This style of EQing gets even more useful as more instruments are introduced into the mix. Think about it this way: every time a new instrument is added into the song, it can affect the clarity of existing elements, due again, to our old friend frequency masking. In many mixes, the bulk of the musical energy resides in the mid-range. This leads to an increased chance of masking in this middle frequency range, often requiring the engineer to put significant attention into EQing tactics to bring back lost clarity and definition.

The genre also affects the likelihood of frequency masking since some styles are typified by particular combinations of instruments and high density. Rock music is the perfect example where distorted electric guitars and heavily compressed drums regularly mask vocals. Frequency masking can be significantly reduced in a song by minimising the number of elements playing simultaneously. Very often, you can add significant clarity to the mix by automating the mute button!

*Every time a new element is introduced into the mix, it can affect the clarity of existing elements*

## Compression or no compression?

For those who prefer to avoid compression in the mix, level automation is an excellent way to achieve a full sounding and balanced vocal. There are some advantages to this approach. For instance, recording directly without any outboard gear simplifies the recording process. It can also yield a very live and 'organic' sound to the recording, mainly if the production goal is to retain this character in the mix.

**The amount of level automation is often dependent on:**

**1. The quality of the performance and recording quality**
Well-played instruments and controlled vocal deliveries often impart a degree of natural levelling, which is captured in the recording.

**2. Dynamics control during recording**
If compression and limiting are used during recording, the automation levelling requirements will likely be minimised during mixing.

**3. The musical genre**
Smaller bands with less instrumentation, and less-dense musical arrangements can effectively reduce frequency masking. This requires less automation to improve clarity and separation in the mix.

**4. The goals of the mixing engineer**
Let's face it: perfection and polish are not always needed on every mix. A radio-friendly pop song most likely needs polished production where a raw-sounding indie release might get much of its inherent character from less processing.

## Combining automation and compression

Combining level automation with compression is a very useful technique for achieving a vocal with a perfect level balance and intelligibility in the mix. But the results very much depend on the order of the compressor and the automation.

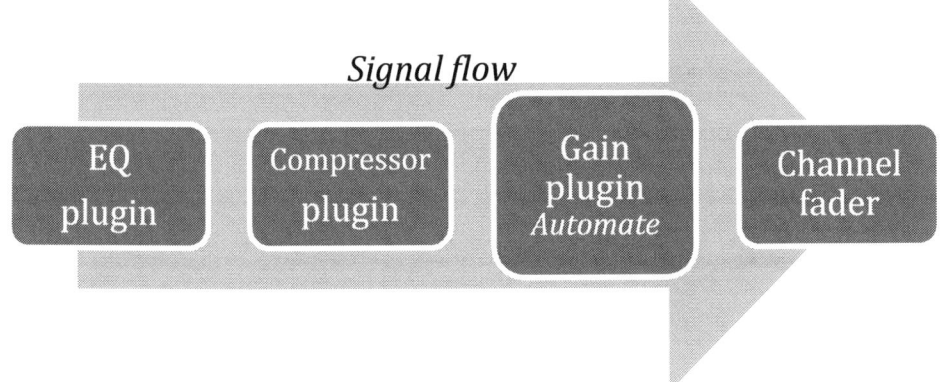

***Image 11: A typical sequence of plugins on a track***
*In this example, the gain plugin takes care of the volume level automation on the track. Adding the gain plugin directly before the track fader allows you to automate volume levels after the dynamics effects while allowing independent control of the track's overall track fader.*

For example, if you automate the level *before* the compressor, the automation has less effect on the resulting output. This is because the compressor will change the level of all your volume level adjustments. This is not the best method for fine-tuning vocal intelligibility. However, the big benefit is that you can feed your compressor with an optimum level so that the compressor is always compressing in its sweet-spot. For instance, those low-level vocal phrases that wouldn't usually trigger the compressor threshold can be raised so that they are now being compressed evenly. Also, the loud phrases that would be over-compressed can be reduced in level for more even compression.

Applying your level automation *after* the compressor enables a far more accurate way to adjust the overall level; even the briefest volume micro-move will yield a noticeable result – not so with the previous method, where significant boosts are sometimes necessary to hear a noticeable change. This method of using level automation after a compressor is an excellent way of getting a great sounding vocal due to the amount of level control available. Regarding the entire vocal plugin chain, the key thing to remember is to add your automation at the end of the chain, just before the channel fader (see image 11 above).

## 2. Creating a relative vocal balance

There are two important considerations when creating a great vocal balance in the mix: it must be consistently levelled, and it must have a good relative balance with other mix elements.

A vocal that is consistently levelled would have all words clearly audible, be intelligible, and avoid level fluctuations in the mix. It might be loud and intense in choruses while being at a moderate level in the verses. But whatever its apparent volume is in each section, it needs to be reasonably consistent. It doesn't matter whether you choose to create consistent levelling with compression only, automation only, or a combination of both, as long as it sounds good.

Again, we come back to the issue of frequency masking where competing musical elements can reduce the intelligibility of the vocal. Your vocal may have a wonderfully consistent level and excellent intelligibility in isolation, but the true test is whether it retains this when combined in the mix. This brings us to the second point.

The second consideration for a great vocal balance is that it must be at a relative level to all other elements in the mix while preserving its clarity and intelligibility. This is the point in the mix process where the vocal will really benefit from fine-tuning adjustments using a series of micro and macro level moves.

## 3. Creating vocal character

Altering the tonal character of the lead vocal is a great way to introduce variation throughout the mix. Character variation is useful because it provides a way to 'freshen' repetitive vocal melodies, avoiding the listener getting bored. These character variations can be anything from subtle to smash-in-the-face obvious; whatever works. They are particularly useful in songs when there is a lot of repetition of melody and phrasing.
Clearly, this approach is in opposition to the idea of maintaining a natural timbre. Therefore, when you mess around with vocal tonality, it needs to make sense in the context of the song. It may work well to add a telephone effect to a backing vocal as it does a call-and-return with a natural sounding lead vocal.

Varying vocal character is also a successful way to signal the listener that a change is about to occur. With this in mind, changing a vocal sound during a transition between two song sections can be very effective.

**Three examples of where to change vocal character in a mix:**

1. To add change during transitions between two song sections, like a verse and chorus, a chorus and middle-8, or a chorus and interlude, etc.

2. To punctuate the end of a vocal melody turnaround during a verse or chorus, e.g. a vocal in a verse could be constructed by two or more repeating phrases.

3. To emphasise a prominent word or phrase.

## Methods to alter vocal tonal character

Some may argue that it's far easier to achieve changes in vocal character in the mix by merely putting the effected vocals on additional tracks. While this method works well it has its negatives: it causes an increase in track count, can cause comb-filtering if your DAW doesn't manage delay-compensation well, and can increase levels because you're adding additional audio, rather than adding effects to one instance of audio.

One good reason for automating effects on a single vocal track is that it allows the engineer the freedom apply and tweak a multitude of subtle effects throughout the mix. This is often easier than continually rendering out words and phrases from the vocal track and applying effects. However, too much automation occurring on one track can get hard to manage. At times, it can make it easier to have separate tracks with vocal effects because it's easier to see and more straightforward to balance in the mix. It often works well to have a combination of both methods, but ultimately, it's up to your preferred way of working.

**Four automation moves that can alter a vocal's tonal character:**

1. Add a reverb plugin to your track and use automation to vary the amount of reverb at different sections in the song.

2. Automate a high pass filter to reduce the low frequencies of a vocal and help add intelligibility in dense parts of the mix.

3. Add an AM radio effect (use a limiter plus an equaliser to limit the bandwidth) to massively change the tone to punctuate poignant words and phrases.

4. Automate a tempo-based delay and vary the effect level during different song sections.

## Summary

1. The main reason to automate the lead vocal is to ensure its clarity and intelligibility in the mix.

2. In many cases, the simplest and most effective method to achieve vocal intelligibility is to automate its volume level before reaching for compression and equalisation.

3. To achieve perfect vocal intelligibility, focus on the vocal elements of articulation by controlling the levels of consonants, nasals, fricatives, sibilants, and vowels.

4. Vocal level automation works well in tandem with a compressor, to create a more levelled sound. Applying automation before or after the compressor makes a difference.

5. You don't always have to use a compressor to level your vocals. For a more natural tone, try using volume level automation only.

6. Automating the lead vocal is an excellent method for injecting character, such as emphasising breaths and consonants.

# seven

## An Automation Scenario

What happens when automation is used across many tracks in a completed mix?

Mix Automation for the Small Recording Studio

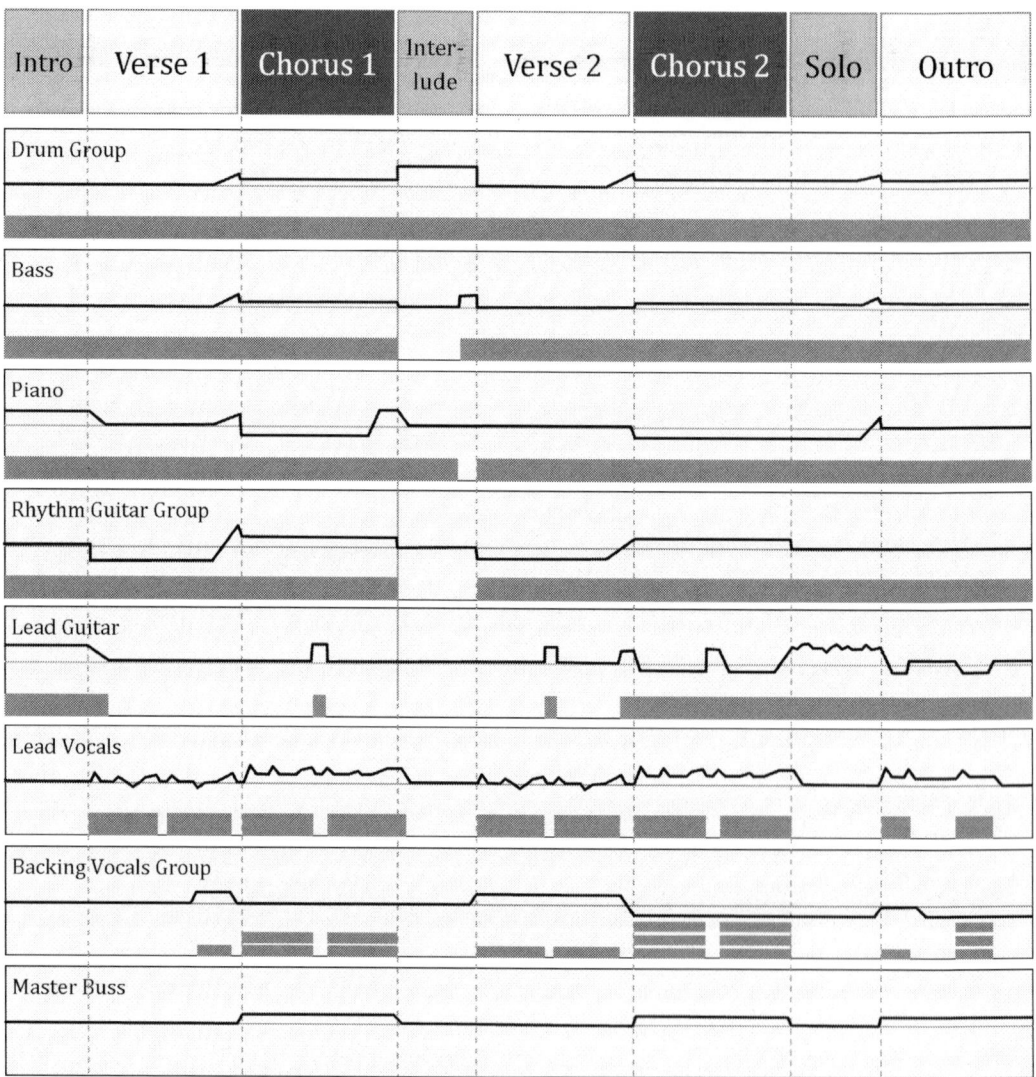

***Image 12: Level automation across multiple tracks and groups in a song***
*Refer to the following overview and explanatory notes for a detailed explanation of the automation done on each track, and how the combination of all automation moves affects the song mix.*

# Overview

This image shows how level automation can be used on multiple tracks and groups to control the dynamics and impact of a complete song mix. Each of the eight rows, or blocks, are either a single track or a group of tracks with each labelled accordingly. For each, a level automation line and a solid-grey bar are shown. The solid-grey bar indicates when a musical element is playing or not playing in the song (e.g. the bass guitar plays for the entire song except in the Interlude). The level automation lines show when the level of the element is raised or lowered. For the backing vocals, each grey bar represents one vocal harmony, giving us a maximum of three backing vocal harmonies at specific points in the song. The master buss is unique because all elements are routed to this track, and a change in level affects the entire mix.

Remember that any automation done on a mix is unique to that song and can be driven by such things as the genre, radio format, performance characteristics, artistic preference, etc. This diagram presents an example of one approach to automating a typical radio-format rock or pop song.

# Explanatory notes

### Intro
The song starts with a typical instrumentation-only intro section.
The lead guitar level is up in the mix so that a robust melodic hook is established at the start of the song. For rhythm elements (piano and rhythm guitars) the piano is emphasised over the guitars so that the song begins with a softer texture. This allows the song to 'build' and have a harder, stronger texture in the choruses. Note how the lead guitar carries on slightly into verse 1 with an automation fade-out to ensure that the last note level is controlled as the lead vocal comes in.

### Verse 1
Interesting things start to happen in verse 1. Note that the automation line for the lead vocal is very wiggly compared to other blocks. This reflects the dynamic changes required to control its level and maintain intelligibility in the mix.

The rhythm guitars' level is reduced so that the piano is the prominent rhythm instrumentation. At the end of the verse, all elements (except the lead guitar) have a ramped increase in level. Note the introduction of backing vocals and the volume ramps creates intensity and signals the listener that something new is about to happen (the chorus). This is called a 'transition'. If you are wondering why the instrumentation levels quickly reduce for some elements when the chorus starts then take a look at the master buss below, where the level of the complete mix is increased.

## Chorus 1
An important feature of the choruses is that the song sounds denser due to more intense performances, more elements occurring, and slightly more level. In this example, the rhythm guitars are emphasised over the piano. The lead vocal level has increased somewhat to retain its prominence, and two-part backing vocals are introduced. Also, the drum group has a small lift to keep it in balance with the rest of the elements. Note the lead guitar acting as a secondary lead (fill) in the gap between the leading vocal phrases. This standard technique helps to maintain energy and momentum in the song. At the end of the chorus, the transition is completed by raising the piano level to emphasise a piano lick.

## Interlude
The interlude introduces a noticeably different sound to the other song sections, being only drums and piano. In this example, the drummer is playing a much softer intensity, so the level automation is used to increase the volume slightly. At the end of the interlude, the transition is completed by emphasising the bass guitar with a small level increase.

## Verse 2
Verse 2 follows very much the same techniques used in verse 1 with some variations added to provide listener interest. In the mix, the engineer uses level automation to raise the volume of the guitar riff to act as a secondary lead element at two locations when the vocalist isn't singing. Secondly, a softly-sung one-part backing vocal harmony is introduced, and the level is raised so that it sounds prominent with the lead vocals.

## Chorus 2
Chorus 2 is very similar to chorus 1 but adds something new for listener interest.

Firstly, the lead guitar is playing a simple melodic phrasing part at a low level but is increased in level at the gap in the lead vocals. Also, note how the level is raised before the end of the chorus to create the transition for the solo section of the song. Secondly, backing vocals are now three-part, and their overall level has been reduced slightly to keep them in balance with the lead vocal. The piano level drops to make the rhythm guitars more prominent.

**Lead guitar solo**
The lead guitar solo has micro volume level automation applied in a similar method to the lead vocal. This is done to raise the level of quiet notes and lower the level of overly prominent notes. Again, the transition into the outro is created by the volume level ramps on drums, bass, and piano.

**Outro**
At the outro, the engineer wants the song to maintain the musical intensity with an 'all guns blazing' outro that leaves the listener with a lasting impression of the song. The very thing that must not happen at this point is that the song reduces in energy. This is done by introducing all the musical elements while using level automation to control the emphasis of the different elements to avoid the outro turning into a big mushy mess. For example, when lead vocals are happening, the lead guitar drops in level, then raises again when the lead vocals stop.

**Master buss**
Level automation on the master buss is done to add impact to the choruses and outro. This is a subtle technique only requires an increase of 0.5 to 1.5 dB (like a good ointment, a little goes a long way). Practically speaking, this involves setting the master fader for the chorus at zero dbFS (full scale) then automating a level *reduction* in the verses.

# eight

## 34 Automation Tips

A summary of tips and techniques for implementing automation into your mix

# General tips

## 1. Check it in the mix
Always make your automation moves with the entire mix running so that the adjustments can be heard in the context of the full mix. It's helpful to solo the element at the start to check that you're altering the parameter that you think you are. At other times, you'll need to solo the element to find the precise location to modify, such as the fricative in a word or a particular note in a distorted guitar solo. For best results, make your final adjustments while the whole mix is playing.

## 2. Automate track levels with a gain plugin
Automate track levels with a separate gain plugin instead of the main fader. This keeps your track level automation independent from your main track fader, enabling you to still alter the track's overall volume without upsetting or rewriting the automation. To do this, ensure your gain plugin occurs immediately before your track fader. Don't underestimate the value of this massively useful tip!

## 3. Use volume level automation as your go-to
There are a variety of different ways to automate elements in the mix, but the simplest and most effective method is volume level automation. Using a combination of micro and macro-moves is hugely effective for emphasising and de-emphasising mix elements, bringing clarity to vocals, and balancing an entire mix.

## 4. Start with the lead vocal
If you're at the stage with your mix where you want to start automating but you don't know where to begin then start with, arguably the most crucial element, the lead vocal. Use micro-moves to control consonants, fricatives, sibilants, and vowels. Then use macro-moves to raise quiet or overly-loud phrases.

## 5. Use a reference song as a guide
If you're new to automation, you may find it difficult to set your targets for what you want automation to achieve in the mix. In the same way that using reference songs are helpful when crafting a mix, they are also useful for crafting character and balance of individual elements. For example, if you're automating your lead vocal then select a song with the vocal sound that you love and try and emulate it.

## 6. Fix an over-compressed recording
Micro-level adjustments can inject life back into over-compressed recordings. For example, with a vocal, consonants and fricatives can be emphasised and sibilance reduced. Compression 'pumping' can also be reduced.

## 7. Draw your curves for greatest accuracy
Manually drawing volume level automation curves with your mouse provides significantly more skill than manually recording fader movements (using the touch/latch/write functionality in most DAWs). While drawing the curves takes longer, it offers far more precision for the shape of the curves and the values that you may be aiming for.

## 8. Identify your automated tracks
If you're working on a mix with a large track-count, it can be a challenge knowing which tracks have automation. To make the automated tracks obvious, include a symbol, like a '+' or '*' in the track names; a glance at the track name will quickly identify the automation tracks. For example, your lead vocal track with automation might be named, '+LVOX' or '*LVOX.'

## 9. Give the choruses more impact
The choruses in a song can be given more impact by slightly raising their overall volume level relative to adjacent song sections. This method involves automating a small level increase on the master fader immediately before the chorus begins, then reducing the fader to its original level directly after the chorus finishes: 1 – 2 dB is usually enough. Ensure you have enough headroom on your master faders so that you can create the increases without causing the overall level to clip.

## 10. Use mutes to create dead-quiet starts and stops in your song

Automated muting is effective at creating perfectly-timed starts and stops to tighten up loosely timed group performances. This technique is very effective for backing vocals, horn sections, and guitars. Alternatively, automating a mute on a group or master buss enables you to have absolutely dead-silent stops during any part of the song. This is useful because even cutting audio clips may not stop reverb and delay effects from ringing on. For example, creating a dead stop on a group of distorted guitars is simple if all of the guitars are routed to a group buss, and you mute the buss. However, if you have guitar reverbs on sends and returns you would need to automate a mute on the effect send.

## 11. Create fades to add vibe and character

Creating automated volume level fades is simple to do and very effective in the mix. You can fade individual elements in or out on a track, or groups of elements on a buss, or create the perfect song fade-out. You can fade in samples to add ambience or adjust the fade-out on a decaying guitar note to remove the accidental fret buzz at the end. Doing a series of consecutive fades enables you to 'swell' the instrumentation in time with the song's tempo. You can also create gentle track or group fader level variations to subtly emphasise and de-emphasise elements in the mix. This is a simply method that requires you to automate volume level fade-ins and fade-outs on the track, group buss, or master buss.

## 12. Panning to reduce frequency masking

Similar sounding elements that occupy the same pan position can suffer from frequency masking. The solution is to automate your panning to reposition the competing elements in the mix panorama. For example, a vocal and guitar could be panned to the centre. Let's say that when the guitar plays rhythm in the verses there is no masking, but when the playing style changes to a strongly melodic arpeggio in the choruses the masking is affecting vocal intelligibility. In this case, you could pan the guitar to a different position during the choruses.

## 13. Panning to create width in the mix

You can create explosive intensity in a mix by narrowly panning sets of elements in a verse, then wide-panning them in the chorus. It is very effective because the instant change from narrow (mono sounding) panning to extremely wide panning can be very dramatic for the listener, adding space and width to the mix. This technique is very effective with mid-range elements like guitars, keyboards, horn sections, and backing vocals and is a classic technique in modern rock and pop music. The method requires you to automate the panning on a selection of individual tracks so that their panning changes from narrow to wide as the song progresses.

## 14. Delay-based effect-swells

Create effect-swells, like reverb and delays, on instruments and groups. A swell is a gradual increase in volume level, with the automation curve looking like a ramp. Effect-swells are a great way to gradually introduce an effect to a voice or instrument in the mix. Alternatively, a repeating delay could be quickly increased from nothing, to provide a heavy effect on the last word of a vocal line. One way to do this is to automate a send level from the track you're working on, to your desired effect. Another method - if your effect plugin is on the track – is to automate the blend (or mix) level of the plugin. But check first, as not all plugins have this feature.

## 15. Automate an equaliser

Dense sections of a song can alter the balance of instrumentation, causing one or more instruments to lose clarity in the mix. This is often caused by masking, which is due to new 'competing' instruments being introduced, or from the sheer volume increase of the overall mix. Automating an equaliser is a great way to bring clarity back to those elements that are losing clarity. It's a great alternative to just raising the level, which can add further imbalance to the mix. The equalisation adjustment can either be a boost, a cut, or a combination of both. For example, let's say a lead vocal has good balance in the verses but loses clarity in the choruses when distorted guitars are introduced due to frequency masking. The engineer automates a small reduction in the 2 – 5 kHz range using a bell curve on a parametric equaliser located on the guitar group buss. Another option is to add a small boost to the same EQ region for the vocal. As mentioned earlier, this approach gives three options: a cut to the guitars, a boost to the vocal, or both. Whatever you do is purely your choice.

A parametric equaliser is usually the best type to use because it gives a variety of filter options: shelving, high-pass/low-pass, and bell. To do this move efficiently requires an equaliser with 'enable' functions for each band. This way, you can pre-set your EQ adjustment, then simply activate and deactivate with automation as needed.

## 16. Automate groups

Whenever possible, automate groups rather than individual tracks. Doing this saves a considerable amount of time, creates consistency, and makes it easier to make changes later. For example, send all your electric rhythm guitars to a guitar group buss, then automate the level of this group buss instead of each individual guitar. Do the same for horn sections, drum kits, keyboard groups, string ensembles, and backing vocals.

## 17. Keep your automation curves visible

It makes sense to keep all of your automation curves visible on the tracks where you've applied them. This makes it easy to see what's happening with your tracks as the mix progresses.

## 18. Move your automated tracks around as you work

The automation you do on one track almost always relates to what's happening on another track. When associated tracks are side by side, it's visually easier to make the necessary adjustments. For example, automating a dip in the level of the guitar group when the lead vocal is singing is easily done when you can see precisely where the vocals are occurring compared to the guitars. Get used to dragging your tracks around to make your automating tasks easier.

## 19. Emphasise transients

A transient is an initial peak at the beginning of a waveform. Raising transients is a great way to inject life back into vocal and instrument recordings that sound flat and lifeless. Reduced transients in a recording are usually due to poor microphone technique, poor performance, or over-compression during recording. Use micro-moves of up to a few dB to raise the levels of these transient peaks and inject punch and excitement back into your mix.

# Vocals

## 20. Improve lead vocal intelligibility in a mix
Create micro-level adjustments to accentuate consonants, fricatives, and esses. This needs to be checked for every word in the song. The amount of correction is dependent on the quality of the recording, what's going on in the mix, and your own goals for how the vocal should sound. It's time-consuming but worthwhile for the clarity that can be obtained.

## 21. Accentuate the tails
The fading note – or tail - of an element can quickly disappear into a mix as its level naturally fades away and gets masked by other mix elements. Where appropriate, raising the tails of these elements in the mix can give a more robust character and increase its prominence in the mix. Examples are a single strummed guitar chord, a sustained vocal vowel, a guitar solo note, and a cymbal hit. These tails can be brought back into the mix by automating a gradual level increase along the length of the tail.

## 22. Control vocal sibilance
Use volume level micro-moves to control the amount of vocal sibilance. While more time consuming than using a de-esser, it is far more accurate because it allows you to target only the offending instances, with precise control over the amount of reduction. Sibilance can also be controlled by automating bell curve dips with an equaliser. However, level control is far more convenient and tends to sound more natural. Remember that esses affect intelligibility, so they still need to be in the mix, but at a controlled level.

## 23. Breath control
Level automation is an excellent method to fine-tune the levels of vocal breaths in a song. While reducing breath levels can help clean up a vocal, raising breath levels can inject a wonderful sense of intimacy into the vocal performance. The main issue to consider is whether the breaths are musical and whether they add value to the song. Again, how much to increase or decrease the level depends on your judgement.

## 24. Automate the level of a vocal into a compressor

Automate the level of a gain plugin before the compressor in your plugin chain. This allows the vocal to be evenly compressed on both quiet and loud parts. It avoids over or under-compression on loud and soft words. This is an excellent trick for achieving very smooth and even compression. Note that this method is less effective at making very obvious level adjustments since the compressor is continually compressing the level increase created by the automation boosts.

## 25. Remove harsh frequencies in a lead vocal

Some singers exhibit nasty resonances on loudly sung notes. For example, female singers can get very resonant in the 2 – 4 kHz region on loud notes. One option is to automate a level reduction at the offending words/phrases. Another way is to automate a parametric EQ plugin, creating a dip in the EQ in that specific region on offending parts.

## 26. Better vocal intelligibility in dense song sections – 1

A vocal can often get lost in dense choruses when one or more competing instruments are causing frequency masking in the upper mid-range, masking vocal fricatives and sibilants. Sustained sounds, like distorted guitars and drum cymbals, are often culprits. One remedy is to use a parametric equaliser plugin and automate gentle boosts to the vocal. Boosts in the 2 - 5 kHz and/or 10 kHz regions utilising a bell filter with a wide Q (width) can work well.

## 27. Better vocal intelligibility in dense song sections – 2

Automating brief volume level boosts to the consonants of words can really improve vocal intelligibility in a dense chorus. It's useful because intelligibility is very much affected by the listener's ability to hear word pronunciation. To be effective, you need to listen carefully to each phrase and apply boosts accordingly, since depending on the performance and the type of consonants, the boosts will vary. Don't just limit yourself to choruses; this technique is fantastic for adding a vibrant intensity to an overall vocal delivery.

## 28. Better vocal intelligibility in dense song sections – 3
For this technique, the goal is to improve lead vocal intelligibility by reducing the masking frequencies from the competing instruments, rather than treating the vocal itself. The advantage is that the natural character of the vocal recording is retained. Using the example of electric guitars, the method involves automating EQ dips in frequency ranges; the 2 – 5 kHz is often very effective, while the 8 - 10 kHz range can improve the clarity of fricatives and sibilants which are essential components of pronunciation. Again, this automation processing should only occur during the song section where the masking is happening and should cease once the song moves to the following less-dense section.

## 29. Vary the reverb on a vocal
Use automation to vary the amount of reverb on a lead vocal. Sometimes, as a song progresses the amount of reverb becomes less audible as the song moves into denser chorus sections. If you set a static reverb level to suit the choruses, it can be overly loud in the verses; setting it for the verses can make it all but disappear in the choruses. The solution is to automate the output level on the plugin. Work out your optimum setting for the verse and the chorus, then create your automation curves to suit.

# Guitars

## 30. Solid rhythm guitars under a vocal
Keep groups of electric rhythm guitars solid and focused in the mix by creating level automation on the group buss. The aim is to have guitars at a slightly lower level under the vocal to retain vocal cl intelligibility while having them louder when the vocal isn't singing. The level difference is often only 1 – 3 dB. To do this, find all the locations in the song where the lead vocal is NOT playing, then create brief level increases in these gaps. The result is that guitars sound very full in the mix.

## 31. Level-balance a guitar solo
This technique enables you to level a guitar solo without using additional compression. This is often very effective, particularly on distorted guitars, where further compression is usually ineffective on highly compressed guitar distortion. Use level automation to raise quiet notes and reduce loud ones. Sustained and decaying notes that fade away into the mix can be raised by automating a level 'ramp' on the tails of the fading notes.

## 32. Reduce string-squeak and more

Volume level automation is an excellent way to reduce occasional and unwanted string-squeaks, fret-buzz, and fret-clanks on electric guitars and basses. Just draw a simple volume level dip over the offending noises.

# Drums

## 33. Use tempo-based automation to enhance a song's groove

Automating volume level swells and panning in time with the song's tempo is a great way to improve a groove. Volume level swells often work better on non-percussive sounds like keyboard pads or big washy soundscapes. Tempo-based panning can be applied to any element, but usually works better on mid-range elements. Be careful with panning foundation elements like drums and bass as this can screw up the balance of your mix. Again, the trick is to automate the panning so that it aligns with the bar and beat markers in your session.

## 34. Emphasise drum elements in a dense mix

Choruses with dense instrumentation can often reduce the clarity of percussion elements in the mix. A classic example is when the kick, snare, and tom hits lose their punch in the mix. A simple remedy is to automate short volume level increases on the drum room mic. For example, in a dense chorus, masked kicks and snares can benefit from a 1 – 3 dB level increase for the entire chorus. Alternatively, raising the prominence of a tom fill may require an increase for the duration of only one bar.

# nine

## Glossary

An explanation of terms and jargon used in this book

### Automation
To automate means to perform a parameter adjustment that usually varies over time. The most common parameter to automate is a track's volume level, but also includes, panning, mute, equalisation, and dynamics and effect plugins.

### Clarity (also Vocal Clarity)
In this book, the term, 'clarity' has been used to describe the tonal characteristic of a musical element. When discussing vocals, clarity is not the same as intelligibility, since while a vocal can have a clear tonal character, it may still lack intelligibility.

### Complementary equalisation
An equalisation technique where adjustments on one musical element have a comparative and opposite adjustment to another, related element. For example, a 2 dB reduction at 2 kHz on one guitar is complemented by a 2 dB increase at 2 kHz on the other guitar.

### Consonant
Consonants are derived from the alphabet and comprise all letters that are not vowels. They include fricatives and sibilants. Regarding mixing and singing, the interest is in how the consonants can be controlled and balanced in the mix so that they provide optimum intelligibility for the listener. In this book, 'consonant' refers to hard sounds, like 'K', 'B', 'P', and medium-sounding consonants, like 'M', 'N', and 'L'.

## DAW
DAW is an acronym for Digital Audio Workstation, meaning the recording and mixing software that is being used on a computer.

## Element
A broad term used for any musical element, e.g. a drum kit, a snare drum, a guitar strum, a lead vocal, a saxophone etc.

## Fricative
A form of 'soft' consonant, such as 'f', 'v', and the 'ch' in the word chapter. The correct term is, 'fricative consonant', but for convenience, this has been simplified to 'fricative' in this book.

## Group
A group is set up by routing selected tracks to another mono or stereo track. This track is often called a 'buss'. This enables the selected tracks to be controlled by the parameters of the group buss, for instance, routing all drum tracks to a 'drum group'.

## HPF (high pass filter)
A high pass filter is a simple equaliser that reduces the low frequencies in a signal. Typically, the 'knee,' or 'roll-off frequency' is adjustable, as is the slope of the filter. Also referred to as a 'low-frequency roll-off.'

## Intelligibility
Intelligibility is about how 'understandable' a word or phrase is and is significantly affected by the prominence of consonants (including fricative consonants and sibilants) and to a lesser degree, the vowel and nasal sounds. In the context of a full mix, vocal intelligibility is mostly affected by its volume level relative to other competing musical elements in the mix.

## In-the-box (ITB)
ITB is a short-hand way of saying that all of your recording and mixing happens in a computer. It is often used to differentiate between working in a computer and working 'out of the box', or on a console.

## Move (Automation)
A 'move' is a way of stating an action when automating a parameter, e.g. an 'automated fader move' describes the recording the adjustment in real-time or drawing in an automation curve in your DAW.

## Sibilant *and sibilance*
A sibilant is a form of consonant that has an 'ess' sound. They are also referred to as 'esses', and are characterised by harsh hissing sounds, such as s, z, sh, and zh sounds. Some consider 'ch' to be a sibilant.

## Song section
This is a general term used for a prominent part in a song's format. Typical examples: intro, verse, chorus, bridge, middle-8, solo, outro, etc.

## Vocal intelligibility
See 'Intelligibility' in this glossary.

## Vowel
In the English language, a vowel sound is any sound that is not a consonant and comprises the letters a, e, i, o, and u, and any combinations of these letters.

# Free eBook
# Free audio examples

To my readers, I'm giving away my FREE eBook,
44 Reasons Your Mixes Suck - And How to Fix Them.
It's packed with common (and not so common) reasons why mixes sound bad and includes a solution for each reason.

Also, I'm giving away high-quality audio files that will give you real examples of some of the automation techniques outlined in this book.

**Please visit:**
**www.mixautomationfreestuff.weebly.com**

# Thanks...

Thanks for purchasing and reading this book.

I hope you found it useful and that it continues to serve as a valuable reference with your future mixing projects.

I would really appreciate it if you could leave me a positive review on Amazon with your honest comments. I read all reviews and use these to make necessary revisions and improvements to this and future books.

Sincerely

Amos Clarke

# Also by this author

Available on Amazon in hard-copy and Kindle formats

---

## Macro-Mixing for the Small Recording Studio
**Produce better mixes, faster than ever using simple techniques that actually work**

Macro-Mixing for The Small Recording Studio, is intended for beginner and intermediate mixing engineers who want to find new ways to massively improve their workflow and the quality of their studio mixes. The book is packed with techniques, examples, guides, and tips to help you create a 'breakthrough' with your mixing. The author includes anecdotes from his own experience working with bands and a range of mixing projects.

---

## 56 Mix Tips for the Small Recording Studio
**Practical techniques to take your mixes to the next level**
AMAZON TOP SELLER

Create magic in your mixes. Flip to any page, read the technique, and apply it. It's really that simple! 56 Mix Tips gets straight into the business of giving you tried and proven mixing tips that actually work. And there's plenty to keep you busy, covering: compression, equalisation, panning, parallel compression, transient manipulation, harmonic distortion, delay-based effects, and so much more. Includes a link to a free online drum processing video tutorial.

# Song Arrangement for the Small Recording Studio
**Practical techniques to take your songs to the next level**

Song Arrangement for the Small Recording Studio explores professional techniques for crafting great sounding music productions that will keep your listeners wanting more. Transform your productions by manipulating Builds, Transitions, Hooks, Groove, Pace, Masking, Lead elements (and much more) in your songs. This book compares many of its techniques to popular radio hits so that you can 'see' them in action.

# 36 Song Arrangement Tips for the Small Recording Studio
**Practical arrangement techniques to take your songs to the next level**

36 Song Arrangement Tips for the Small Recording Studio is the perfect compilation of song arrangement tips and techniques that will help you create great music productions. This book has similar content to the author's other book, Song Arrangement for the Small Recording Studio, but is formatted into an easy-to-read, tips-based reference (with brand new techniques) that is a perfect studio companion for the songwriter, producer, and mixing engineer. Includes links to free online material.

Printed in Great Britain
by Amazon